NO LONGER PROPERTY OF
SEATTLE PUBLIC LIBRARY

# FACE BUG

Poems by
J. Patrick Lewis

Photographs by
Frederic B. Siskind

Illustrations by
Kelly Murphy

WORDSONG

AN IMPRINT OF HIGHLIGHTS

Honesdale, Pennsylvania

## ON EXHIBIT

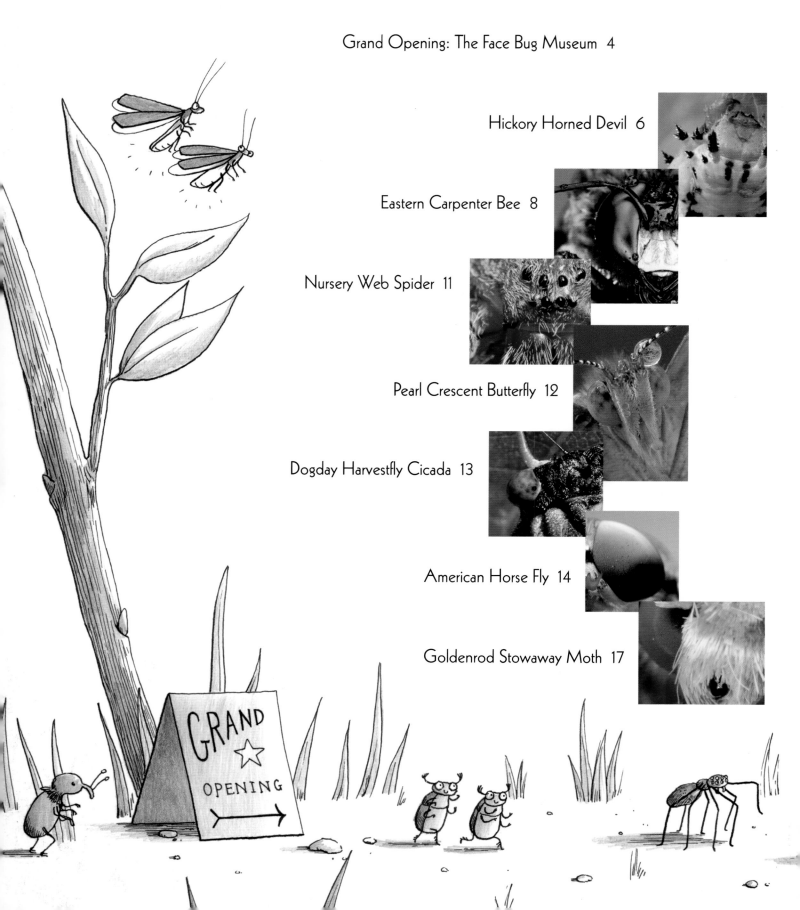

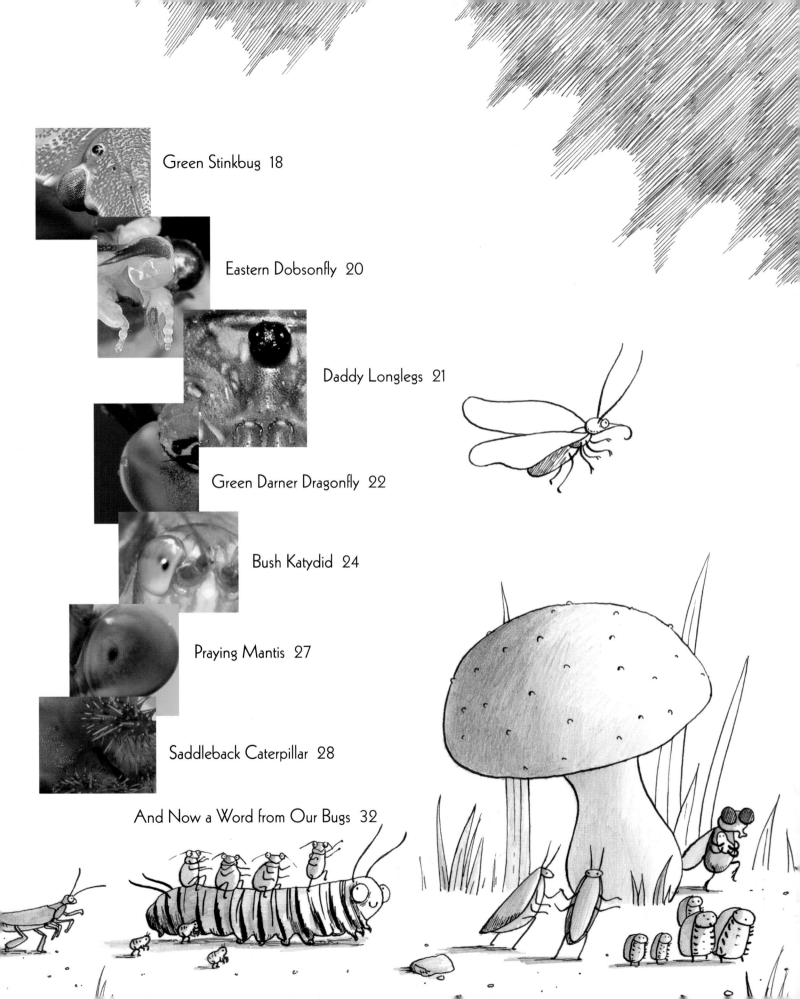

# Grand Opening: The Face Bug Museum

Climb through windows, walls, or basement, Insects, Spiders, guests. It's free!
Our Smithsonian—from Dragon-, Horse-, and Butterfly to Bee—
Is a hoppin', bug eye-poppin' photo show. The place is packed!
We've installed designer lighting for the Moths it will attract.

You may think you've seen our Show Bugs in the trees or in the sky,
But you never really know bugs till you look them in the eye.
Are you Spider writers ready? Cast your vote for FAVORITE BUG.
Cameras welcome. Penny postcards of each fascinating mug.

Staring at these scary photographs can cause *Insecto-shock*.
But don't worry, Tiny Vet is standing by around-the-clock.
Stale refreshments? Aphid burgers, leaf decay, swamp water, too!
Oh, believe me, THE FACE BUG MUSEUM's looking out for you.

No antennae on the photos, pests. Just come and face your fear.
Drop whomever you are eating. Our Grand Opening is here!

VISIT THE
*Gift
Shop!*

# Hickory Horned Devil

*Citheronia regalis*

*Look!* A mini porcupine,
Country-colored coral reef
On an overhanging leaf,
Mother Nature's Frankenstein

Nonchalantly eats his fill.
What if you were just a small
Caterpillar, one inch tall,
Who met this Devil dressed to kill?

He would never hurt a flea.
But when he begins that whole
Lazy alligator roll
Upside down, you'll wish that he

Grabbed a different leaf to chew,
'Cause no matter what he does,
Six-inch Devil scares the fuzz
Off a one-inch bug like you.

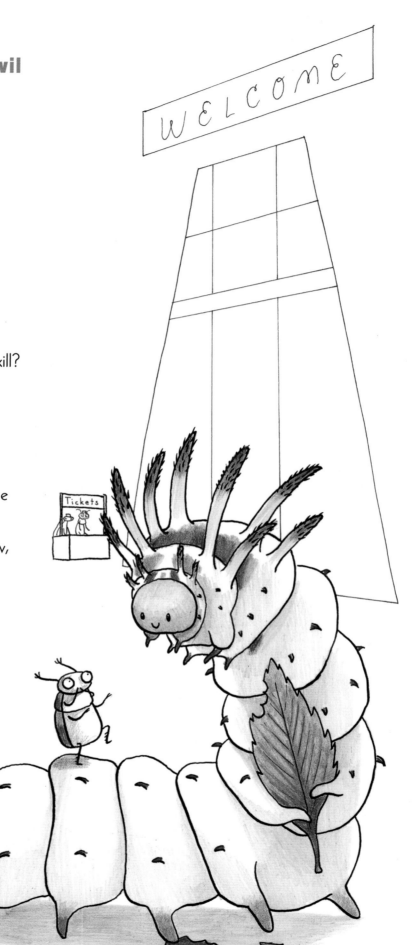

The Gentle GIANT

Inches 0 1 2 3 4 5 6

ARE YOU AS LONG? MEASURE + SEE!

I'm stuck!

# Eastern Carpenter Bee

*Xylocopa virginica*

Who has made a hole in your house,
A hole in your house?
That's me!
It's what I learned to do in school.
You see, I'm a *carpenter* bee.

I may look as mean as a beetle
With a face that
People dread,
But I need to infest to nest and rest
My football-helmet head,

If not in a house, then a condo
Or apartment,
A room rent-free,
A neighborhood where the wood's so good
It tastes like Vitamin Bee.

THE *Master* CARPENTER

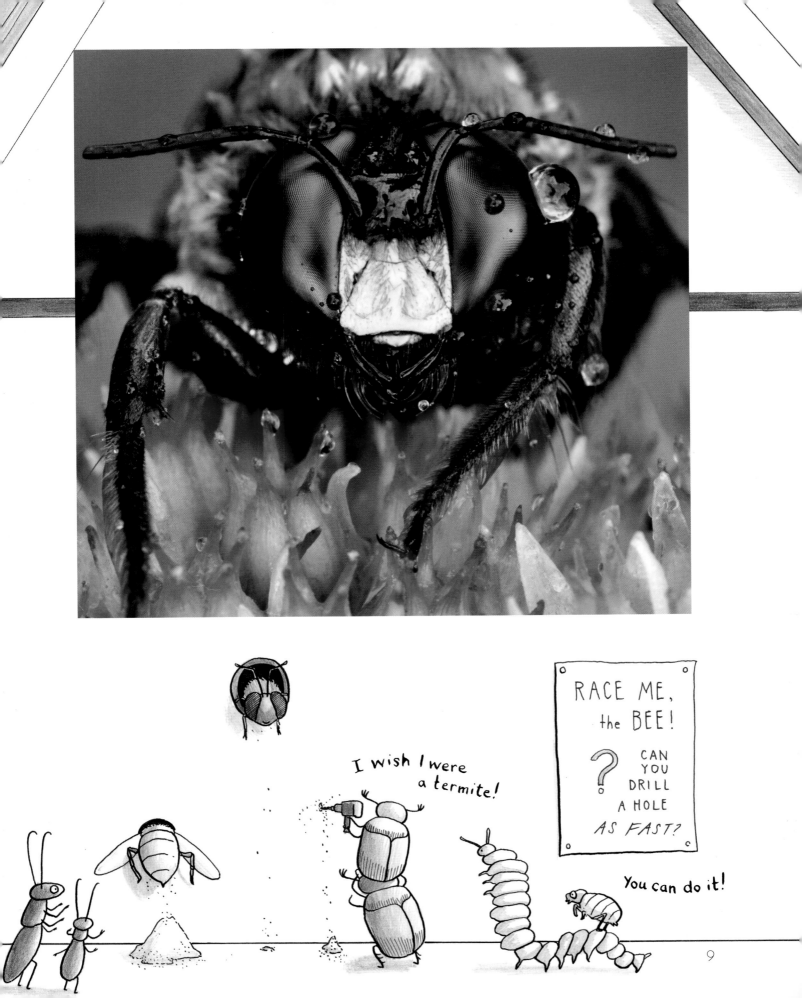

# Nursery Web Spider

### Genus *Pisaurina*, **several species**

Eight black eyes in a whiskery face,
Eight round eyes in a dark crawl space
That never bother blinking back
Could give a kid a heart attack!

Before the male and female mate,
He offers her a gift—a fly,
A flea, or moth—can you guess why?
(So she won't put HIM on her plate!)

But unlike many of her kind,
The Nursery Web takes in her jaws
Her egg sac tenderly because
By evolution, she's designed

To build a sort of nursery "tent"—
A wide-eyed spider bride event!—
And puts her eggs inside to hatch,
Then stands guard by her motherbatch.

Wee!

Look, Ma!
No hands!

They're
so cute!

## Pearl Crescent Butterfly

*Phyciodes tharos*

Sipping on a black-eyed Susan—
Any
    flower
        nectars
            ooze
                in
(Have to have my Insect Ale!)—
I am one Pearl Crescent male,
Perfect match for a million cousins,
Multiplying by the dozens.

If it's summer, here they come,
Females
    smaller
        than
           a
              thumb,
Laying eggs on aster plants.
Sister Pearl, if there's a chance
I should fall asleep, would you
Kindly brush away the dew?

The Nectar Café

TODAY!
Sample
Pearl Crescent's
*favorite*
flavors!

We have
black-eyed
Susan!

I'd love a fresh drop
of nectar.

# Dogday Harvestfly Cicada

*Tibicen canicularis*

Bug's one ugly
Nut to crack.
Is that Bugly's
Front or back?

What?! *Two* faces
On this mutt?
Creepy. Never
Mind his butt.

Front or top view,
What the heck?
He's a head-on
Insect wreck.

Go on, touch him—
All he does
Is ask, "*Who's there?*"
In wonder-buzz.

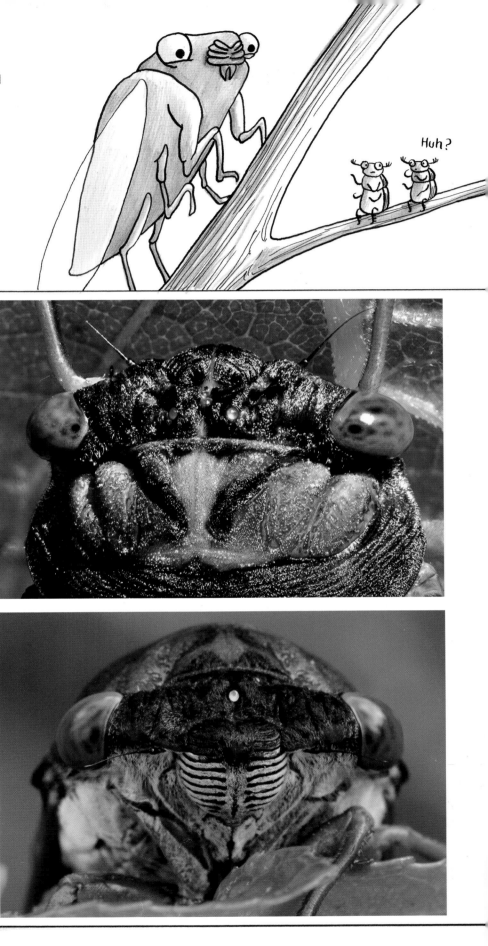

# American Horse Fly

*Tabanus americanus*

This Clydesdale of all flies
Has one long drip syringe
And several thousand eyes
That make her victims cringe.
She polishes her spear
To poke you with it, kid:
Your horse fly souvenir
Becomes a pyramid.

# Goldenrod Stowaway Moth

*Cirrhophanus triangulifer*

Startled by her beauty, I
Bend down and whisper, "Hello."
A moth has perched upon a flower,
     A "goldenrod," bright yellow.

A fine disguise that's perfect for
A "stowaway" to blend in
And miss a swallow's mouth a moth
     Would never want to end in.

But there are, oh, one hundred twenty
Things I would not dare do,
And one is touch a bristle on
     That paintbrush of a hairdo!

To win her heart, a boy moth knows
He really must impress her,
And so he makes appointments at
     The Front Porchlight Hairdresser.

The
*Master*
of
DISGUISE

CAN YOU FIND
THE STOWAWAY?

Whoa!
Glamour
camouflage!

17

# Green Stinkbug

*Chinavia hilaris*

*P.U.!* I found an insect
Who has uncommon scents.
Hello there, Mrs. Stinkbug,
My nose is your defense.

You're good at looking harmless,
And go about your day
Enjoying Mother Nature . . .
Unless I'm in your way.

If I don't keep my distance
Around your flower bed,
You'll turn the little switch on
Your dial, *Full Steam Ahead.*

Yes, you're the clever creature
That everybody thinks
Is quite a thing of beauty,
But sometimes beauty stinks.

HONEYSUCKLE!

LILAC!

GUESS THAT SMELL

GASP!

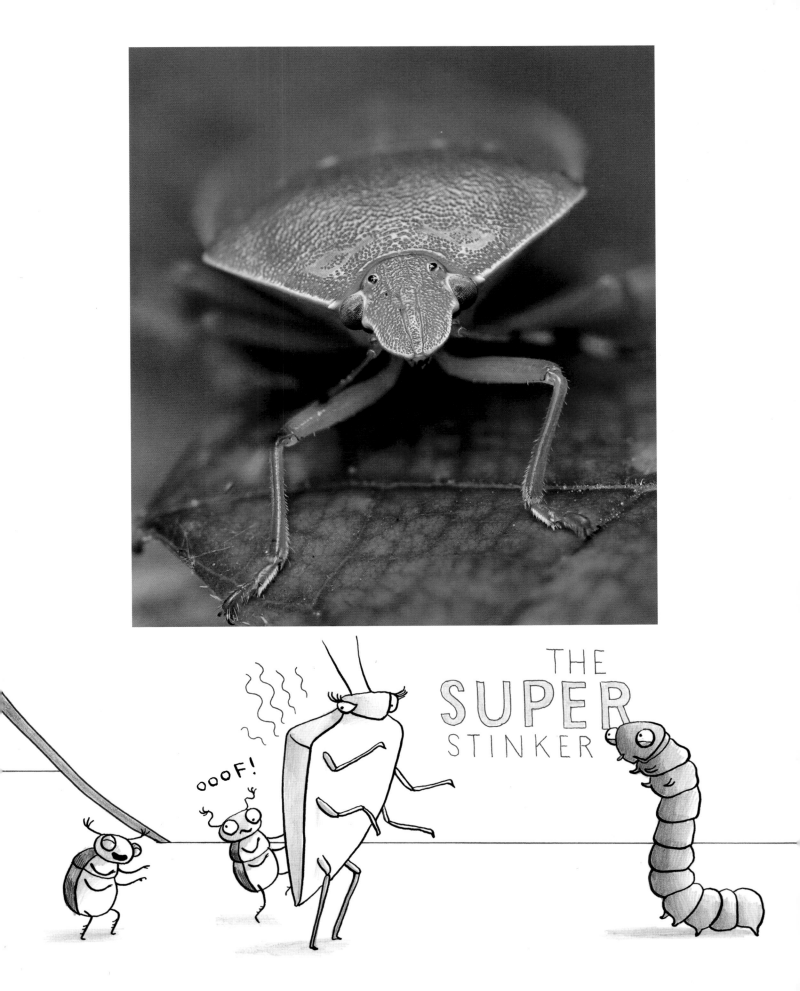

THE SUPER STINKER

OOOF!

# Eastern Dobsonfly

*Corydalus cornutus*

I love you, Mr. Dobsonfly.
Why?

    Because of your huge mandible!
    (Understandable)
    Because your life is mostly larval.
    (A river marvel)
    Because of those bucktooth incisors.
    (Your hypnotizers)
    Because you live the life aquatic.
    (How exotic!)
    And
    There's
    Another
    Reason
    Why—
        Because I'm *Mrs.* Dobsonfly.

20

## Daddy Longlegs

*Phalangium opilio*

My head is brown and shiny,
My eyes are black and tiny.
    Granddaddy says I'm cute.

My eight legs work like wires,
My mouth's a pair of pliers.
    Don't I look like a hoot?

My days are slow and quiet.
I usually watch my diet—
    And always watch my back.

Of course, I like to pitter-
Patter till some critter
    Approaches—Daddy's snack!

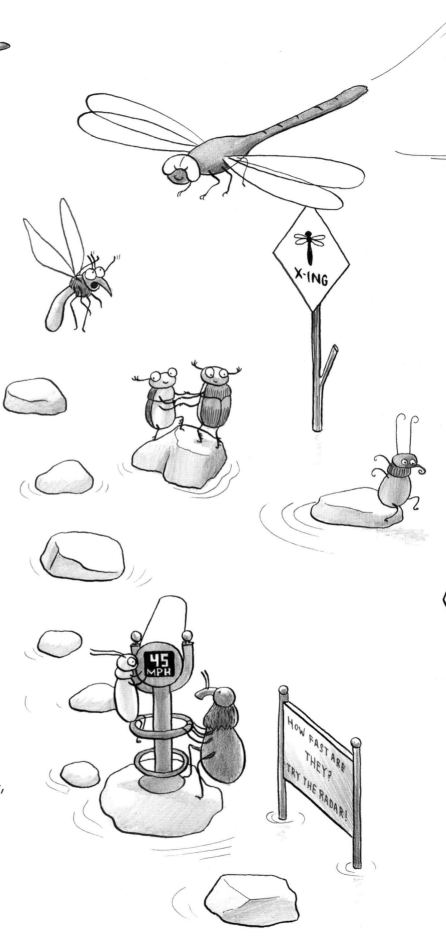

## Green Darner Dragonfly

*Anax junius*

Helicopter Dragonflyer
Stopping, starting rapid-fire.
He's the Emperor of the Pond,
Skimming lily pad and frond.
Day is sunny, but he's shady,
Spots a Darner Dragon Lady.

Dragonflyer helicopter,
How his victory would have stopped her,
She, the sweetheart of the chase.
But he had to feed his face,
So our Dragonfly torpedo
Swerved for lunch—a fat mosquito!

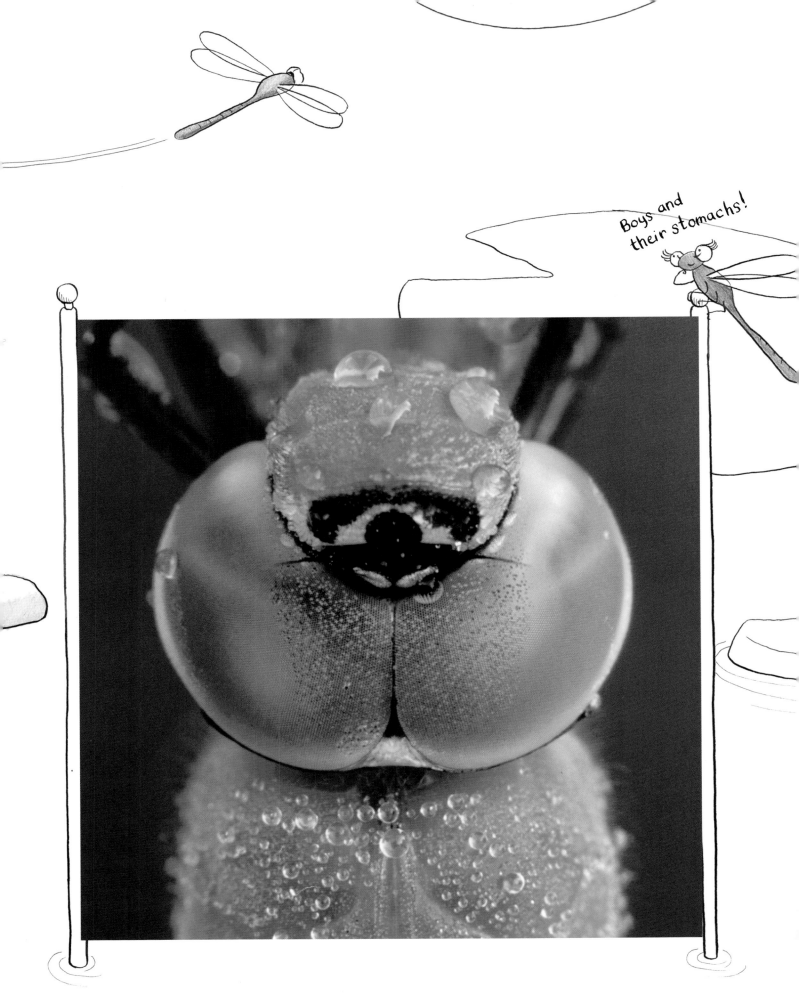

Boys and their stomachs!

# Bush Katydid

Genus *Scudderia*, several species

In England, I'm *bush-cricket*,
But *katydid* to a Yank.
To humans who don't know me,
I'm just a blankety-blank.

To a mirror, I'm a grasshopper.
To an enemy, a leaf.
To an elm tree, I'm a singer.
To a shrub, a petty thief.

To an orange, I say, "Hey, breakfast!"
On tree bark, I grow fat.
To sunlight, I'm a magnet.
To windshields, I'm a . . .

## splat!

His wings make beautiful tunes.

The Amazing Wing Singer

TONIGHT'S PERFORMANCE

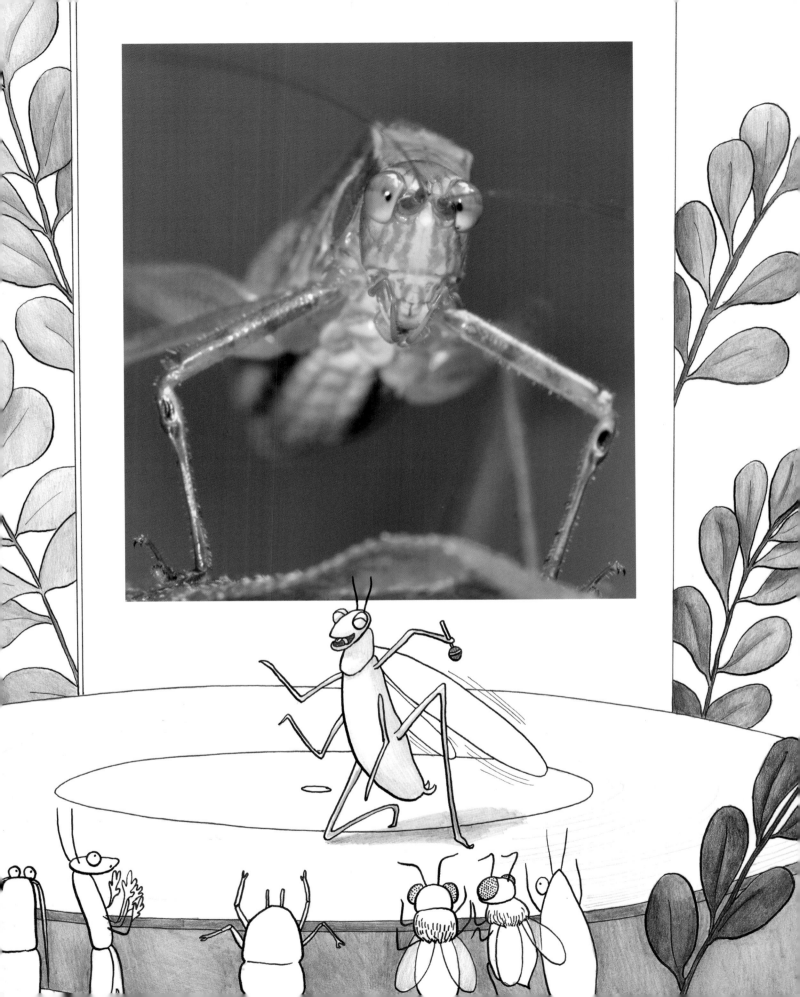

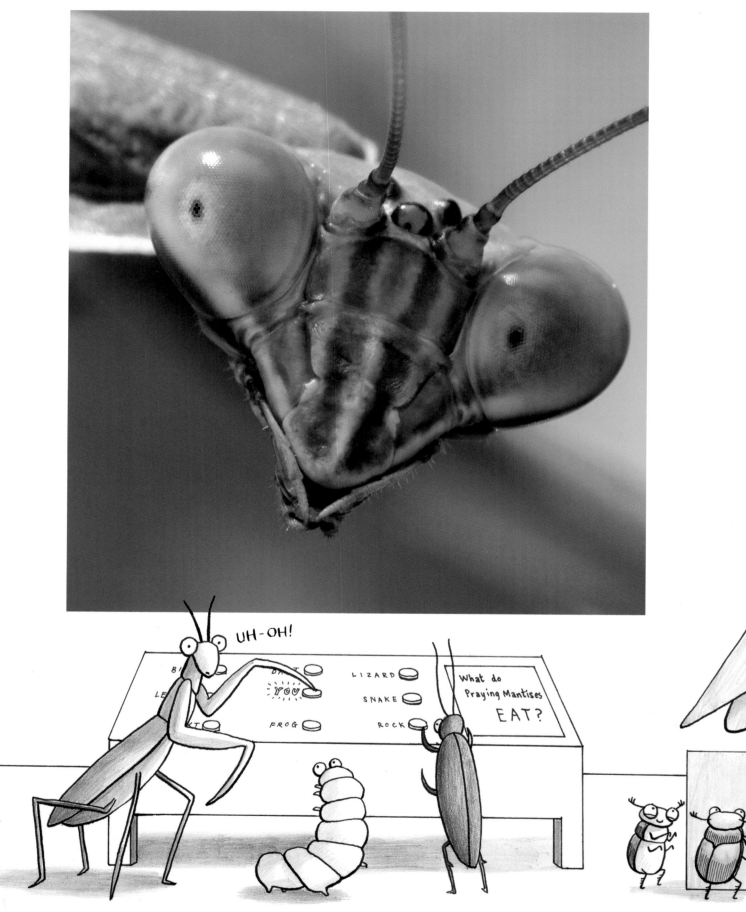

## Praying Mantis

Chinese Mantid, *Tenodera aridifolia*

Great gobs of ghastly beasts are flung
Across the forest. There among
　　　The greenery,
　　　Quite patiently,
The paper-thinsect stares.
That look—what is it meant to show?
She's starring in a video?
She's piloting a UFO?
　　　Could she be saying prayers?

Her prayers are answered. "Look who's here—
My kind of male! Now be a dear,
　　　Play piggyback,
　　　You mant-iac."
He's caught! What can he say?
Her gruesome jaw unbolts to bite
Him. "Oh," he says, "it's our first fight . . .
Are you always this impol—?"
　　　But he is bug fillet.

THE
*PATIENT*
PREYER

That statue looks so real!

27

# Saddleback Caterpillar

*Sibine stimulea*

Though kids love him in Room 102,
There's a horrible hullabaloo
    When the substitute teacher
    Says, "Children, that creature
Belongs in a non-petting zoo.

"He's handsome, he's graceful and cute,
But a bug in a mo' hair suit
    Can tenderly stroke you
    Or suddenly poke you—
A saddleback rash is a beaut!"

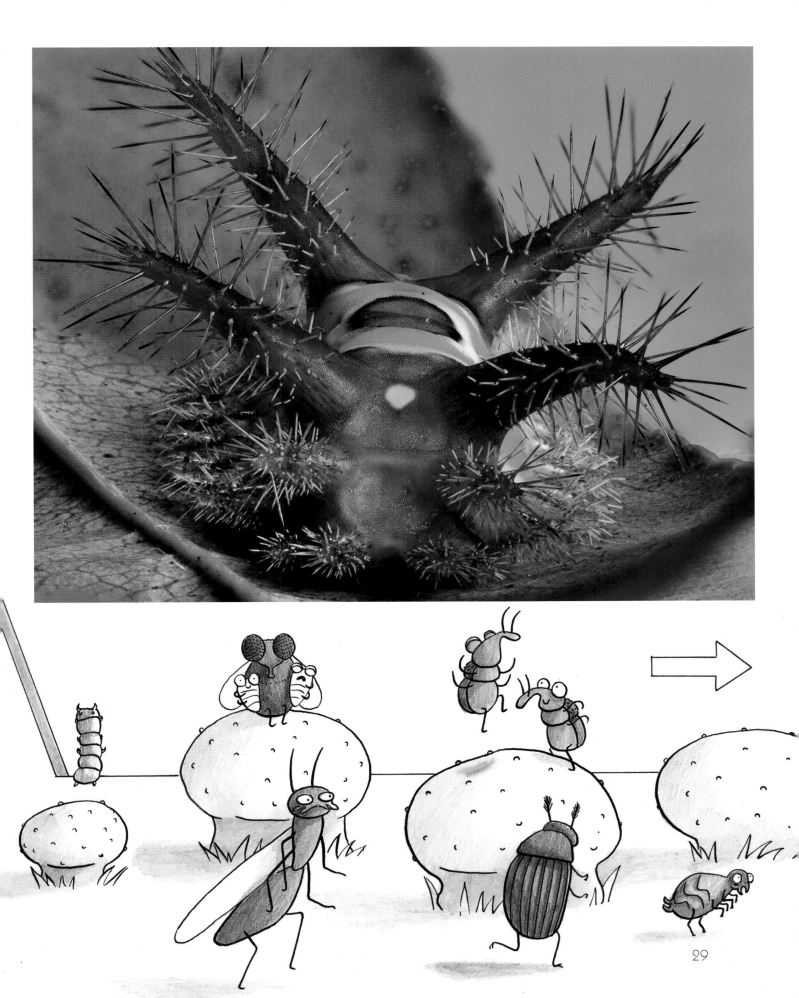

# AND NOW A WORD FROM OUR BUGS

## Hickory Horned Devil

WHERE I LIVE: Hot weather makes me giddy! That's why I live mostly in the Deep South, though I've been known to crawl as far north as New York and as far west as the eastern parts of Kansas.

HOW I GROW: I'm the larva of the Royal Walnut Moth (or Regal Moth). On page 7, you'll see a picture of me as a child before I spread my wings. I may look like a six-inch dragon, but unless you're a leaf, I don't bite.

WHAT I EAT: I feed for about forty days on walnut, hickory, lilac, sycamore, sumac, and sweet gum leaves. In late summer, I burrow underground and spend the winter as a pupa, growing into an adult moth. No spinning cocoons for me; they're for the birds!

WHAT EATS ME: Let's just say my best friends do *not* include hungry feathered fiends.

## Eastern Carpenter Bee

WHERE I LIVE: I'm an East Coast kind of bee, but you can also find me in the Midwest.

HOW I GROW: My mom put pollen and nectar (yum!) in her nest, then laid her eggs on top. I spent the winter growing up in the same tunnel where I hatched. Except for my shiny, black tummy and fuzzy underparts, I look like a bumblebee. I don't have a stinger, though my sisters do. But why bother stinging human pests, anyway?

WHAT I EAT: Flower nectar, of course.

WHAT EATS ME: Hooligans who'd love to gulp me include robber flies, kingbirds, mockingbirds, woodpeckers, and huge dragonflies.

## Nursery Web Spider

WHERE I LIVE: Worldwide, nearly 300 species of us nursery web spideys reap what we sow—oops—I mean sew. In North America, we spin down from Quebec to Florida, even out west to Kansas. Look for me in damp spots, like woods and meadows—and maybe even your basement?

HOW I GROW: I began life as a little egg in a sac attached to my mother's jaw. When it was almost hatching time, she stitched the sac to a plant and built a tent around it. Under mother's watchful eye, we spiderlings stayed in the tent until we were big enough to set off on our own.

WHAT I EAT: Tadpoles and insects would be my first choice, if I can catch them. Usually I have to be satisfied with scraps and whatever I can find that's smelly and edible.

WHAT EATS ME: Sometimes we hungry girl Nursery Web Spiders eat our mates. *Whew*—lucky for me I am not a boy! I can jump six inches—if the wind's with me—to escape from a wasp, bird, or amphibian.

## Pearl Crescent Butterfly

WHERE I LIVE: Wherever beauty is in great demand! You can find me in pastures, vacant lots, and piney woods in every part of the U.S. (except the West Coast), Mexico, and Canada, especially Ontario.

HOW I GROW: On the underside of a host plant, I hatched from an egg with a bunch of other caterpillar babies. I fed on asters before forming a brownish chrysalis.

WHAT I EAT: Now, in my butterfly life, I drink nectar from a whole garden of wildflowers, including dogbane, swamp milkweed, shepherd's needle, asters, and winter cress.

WHAT EATS ME: I count robber flies, spiders, mantises, and, of course (like so many of my friends in this museum), BIRDS on my Most Scary List.

## Dogday Harvestfly Cicada

WHERE I LIVE: I get my name, "dogday," from the warm dog days of late summer. My middle name, "harvestfly," again tells you when I'm around—at the end of the season, harvest time. Listen for my song (but only during the day) in southern Canada and the eastern U.S. Our girlfriends don't sing, but we cicada boys serenade them with music that sounds like an electric saw cutting wood!

HOW I GROW: After mating, my mom cut open a twig and laid her eggs. We hatched in about six weeks. I became a nymph and burrowed into the ground, sucking juice from tree roots for about three years. Then I started climbing my host tree. Halfway up, I lost my outer skin, emerging as an adult cicada. No, not one of those cicadas that appears in 13- or 17-year cycles. You can see cicadas like me each summer. If a robin announces spring, a cicada is a reminder that autumn is only about a month away. My big, green compound eyes and red single-cell eyes are cool, aren't they? Look at me from the top to see all five eyes (top photograph on page 13) or head-on from the front—where mainly the compound eyes are visible—to see my other face (bottom photograph on page 13).

WHAT I EAT: As a grown-up, nothing, because we cicadas have such very short adult lives. So I get to *not* eat, *not* drink, and be merry while looking for a female cicada.

WHAT EATS ME: Here's the deal: I love to trill to attract a female, but I hate that my melody is also a dinner bell to enemies, like copperhead and garter snakes, cicada killer wasps, birds, squirrels, and opossums.

## American Horse Fly

WHERE I LIVE: Unlike some of my cousins who were born in a ditch or a sluggish stream, I grew up in a farm pond. There are about 100 species of us in the genus *Tabanus* in North America, so we make one big, rowdy family of rotten pests!

HOW I GROW: Quickly . . . and to a length of anywhere from ¾ of an inch (like me) to 1⅛ inches (like my tallest brother). Mom hangs her egg mass on a plant that leans over fresh water. As larvae, we dive in the mud and stay for two winters, becoming pupae (adolescents, sort of) in spring. Males die quickly, but I may survive until the fall.

WHAT I EAT: For breakfast, lunch, or dinner, I find that the juicy rear end of a horse can't be beat. The horse may feel like it's having blood drawn with a tiny pair of scissors. But the swish of a pony's tail won't stop me for long! My brothers feed only on nectar.

WHAT EATS ME: Birds and frogs are on my short list of meanies. Guess who the scariest predator is? YOU, flyswatter kid!

## Goldenrod Stowaway Moth

WHERE I LIVE: Perched on or hiding in a goldenrod or sunflower, that's where you'll find me, mostly in the eastern U.S., though I'm fairly rare. I fly mainly in August and September.

HOW I GROW: If you saw me as a caterpillar (brown with a light stripe down my back), what amazing changes from larva (caterpillar) to pupa to . . . *voilà*! Who would guess I'd become a beautiful stowaway moth?

WHAT I EAT: As a caterpillar child, I feed on Spanish needles—also known as beggarticks—black jack, burr marigolds, and sunflowers. But once I transform into a moth, I'm like a kid in a candy shop— I mean candy *flower*. My mouth parts let me slurp liquids, like nectar. Solids in my diet? None for me, thanks.

WHAT EATS ME: My gold and yellow coloring provides me with excellent camouflage among the goldenrod flowers, but I can't always escape from spiders, birds, and ambush bugs.

## Green Stinkbug

WHERE I LIVE: Inspect your orchard, garden, or crop fields throughout North America—or just breathe deeply—and you'll know . . . I'm *baaack!*

HOW I GROW: I come from a keg-shaped egg, attached to the underside of foliage. Growing up, I have one goal: to out-stink a skunk.

WHAT I EAT: With my little needle-like mouthparts, I feed on the juices of plants from May till the first frost. By the time I'm an adult, I'm famous for my odorific talents, as well as for being a farmer's pest. Tomatoes, beans, peas, cotton, corn—almost anything that contains seeds—suit my taste.

WHAT EATS ME: If you're a bird, wood frog, praying mantis, Green Darner Dragonfly, or spider wanting to crunch me, beware! I'll douse you with foul-smelling liquid from the large stink glands on the underside of my thorax.

## Eastern Dobsonfly

WHERE I LIVE: You never heard of a dobsonfly? There are 100 species, more or less, though only a small handful of us live in the New World; the rest are in Africa, Asia, and Australia. I don't suppose you've ever heard of a fishfly, either. Fishflies are my closest relatives.

HOW I GROW: I can be up to 5 inches from pincer tips to wingtips. For most of my life, I'm a larva called a hellgrammite (also "go-devil" or "crawlerbottom"), a favorite bait of "hook-'em Henrys" (fishermen rascals). Once I've become a pup (okay, a "pupa"), I overwinter in a cocoon. Then I crawl out to mate. After two or three years as a larva, I live as an adult for seven days, more or less! Pretty nifty, eh? I get to spend almost my whole life never having to grow up or grow old.

WHAT I EAT: As a 2-inch to 3-inch larva, I snatch nearly anything that swims by, including other aquatic insects—even small fish. In adulthood, I don't live long enough to eat. Focusing only on finding a mate, I live on love.

WHAT EATS ME: When I'm a larva, fish and crayfish find me tasty. Later on, I'm prey to raccoons and bullfrogs, or anything big enough to handle Megaloptera ("large-winged insects").

## Daddy Longlegs

WHERE I LIVE: Oh, I may look like a spider, however I really belong to the order Opiliones. I'm an eight-legged arachnid but not a spider. Though only 150 species of us call the U.S. and Canada home, we win an Olympic medal for Insect Globe-Trotting, since 7,000 (!) species of us leggy wonders slow-foot it on every continent but Antarctica.

HOW I GROW: Mommy daddy longlegs lay their eggs in autumn in the soil or in cracks in wood. We hatch in the spring. Young daddy longlegs are called "leatherjackets" because of our hard outer shell, which we must shed regularly to grow. In the northern U.S., we live only a year, but in the Southeast— I'm a Tennessean myself—we can overwinter for up to two years.

WHAT I EAT: I relish any small invertebrate, preferably an aphid or a spider. Usually, though, I have to resort to scavenging for dead insects, food waste, or vegetable matter.

WHAT EATS ME: I'm not venomous, but the scent glands attached to my hips help scare predators. If that doesn't work, I can always detach a bitten leg as I'm running away. And if *that* doesn't work, I'm out of luck: a bird like a starling will be feeding me to her young.

## Green Darner Dragonfly

WHERE I LIVE: If you're in Washington State, look for me, the Official State Insect. But darners also fly all over North America and as far south as Panama and the Caribbean, not to mention Asia.

HOW I GROW: Mom lays her eggs beneath the water's surface. As nymphs, we are aquatic carnivores, but we have to move fast to catch tadpoles, insects, and small fish.

WHAT I EAT: I'm one of the biggest dragonflies around, named for my resemblance to a darning needle. My meals are always take-out: I catch insects in mid-flight, including moths, mosquitoes, and flies.

WHAT EATS ME: Maybe you've noticed that I'm an extremely agile pilot? Still, I can be caught by a dive-bomber or a quick-tongue—birds, lizards, frogs, spiders, and even larger dragonflies.

## Bush Katydid

WHERE I LIVE: I belong to one of over 100 species of katydids in the U.S., and some 6,000 species worldwide, mostly in tropical countries. Sometimes called a "long-horned grasshopper," I'm more closely related to a cricket, only prettier. But you knew that, right?

HOW I GROW: I hatched from an egg that my mother laid under the leaf of a plant. And over hundreds of generations, we katydids evolved to look very much like leaves ourselves!

WHAT I EAT: I'm a foliage-loving vegetarian, but some of my cousins prefer to dine on insects.

WHAT EATS ME: You have to have a sharp eye to catch me! When it comes to being a mimic and wearing camouflage, I'm the expert of the insect kingdom. Still, somehow critters like mantises, birds, wasps, spiders, frogs, and bats sometimes seize my cousins and me anyway—it must be by sheer luck, though!

## Praying Mantis

WHERE I LIVE: Hot and cool climates suit me just fine. I'm one of some 2,200 species of mantises the world over, but there are only about 20 in the U.S. Can you guess where my nickname, "Praying Mantis," comes from? Yep, my motionless, prayer-like stance.

HOW I GROW: I go through three stages: egg, nymph, and adult. Several hundred siblings and I all hatch at once in the spring. We molt several times—"growing pains," you might say. Then we mate, and I will lay more eggs before my generation dies in autumn.

WHAT I EAT: Yes, it's true. What can I say? I have a fondness for eating my mate after mating. And have you noticed my swivel head? I can turn it nearly 180 degrees. Better to see you with, my dear. Plus it gives me a great view of the Insect Cafeteria.

WHAT EATS ME: Excuse me! Don't listen to Bush Katydid. I am a queen of camouflage, though I must be a tasty dish because owls, bullfrogs, chameleons, and milk snakes sometimes see through my disguise.

## Saddleback Caterpillar

WHERE I LIVE: A native of eastern North America, I wear a prominent, white-ringed brown dot in the middle of my back. It must look like a saddle to you, because that's how I got my name.

HOW I GROW: Mother lays her eggs on the leaves of a plant in clusters of thirty to fifty. I'll mosey around as a caterpillar for four to five months, eating, sleeping too, especially after shedding my skin. Then I'll spin a silk cocoon and lose my caterpillar cuteness to become a dark brown, fat-bodied moth. Isn't Mother Nature strange?

WHAT I EAT: Just about anything that appears in front of me, such as maple, holly, oak, and dogwood tree leaves, as well as hackberry, blueberry, and spicebush. My motto: will crawl for food.

WHAT EATS ME: You would think that flashy me would attract many predators, but they've learned that my horns on both ends, like the hairs on my body, secrete a venom that is, uh, nauseating. And the "face" on my bottom looks more like a face than the face on my face! Egad, I've confused myself. Anyway, I could wear a sign on either end of me: "Go away, if you know what's good for you!"

The "face" on my bottom

For Mary Gifford Hearley
—JPL

For Elena and Vlad
—FBS

For Josie, the brother who enjoyed bugging me
—KM

*The bugs and I would like to thank photographer extraordinaire Fred Siskind, not only for the museum portraits,*
*but for his compound eye in weeding the text for any errors, and Kelly Murphy for her*
*grand and graphic illustrations of the bugs at play.*
*—J. Patrick Lewis*

Face Bug
Text copyright © 2013 by J. Patrick Lewis
Photographs copyright © 2013 by Frederic B. Siskind
Illustrations copyright © 2013 by Kelly Murphy
All rights reserved
For information about permission to reproduce selections from this book,
contact permissions@highlights.com.

The publisher thanks John L. Capinera, PhD, chairman of the Entomology Department
at the University of Florida, for reviewing the text, photographs, and drawings
for this book.

WordSong
An Imprint of Highlights
815 Church Street
Honesdale, Pennsylvania 18431
wordsongpoetry.com
Printed in Mexico

ISBN: 978-1-59078-925-4
Library of Congress Control Number: 2012943510

First edition

10 9 8 7 6 5 4 3 2 1

Designed by Barbara Grzeslo
Production by Margaret Mosomillo
The text of this book is set in Kabel.
The drawings are done in ink and graphite.